A Kalmus Classic Edition

Antonio
VIVALDI

D1546706

SONATE DA CAMERA A TRE

Opus 1

Book One: Sonatas I–VI

FOR TWO VIOLINS AND CELLO (BASSO CONTINUO)

K 04786

SONATE DA CAMERA A TRE

Sonata I

Antonio Vivaldi, Op. 1

4

ALLEMANDA
Allegro

CAPRICCIO

GAVOTTA
Allegro

Sonata II

CORRENTE
Allegro

GIGA

Allegro

GAVOTTA

Allegro

Sonata III

ALLEMANDA
Allegro

SARABANDA

Sonata IV

ALLEMANDA

SARABANDA

GIGA

Sonata V

PRELUDIO

ALLEMANDA

Presto

CORRENTE
Allegro

GAVOTTA
Presto

Presto

Sonata VI

PRELUDIO
Grave

CORRENTE
Allegro

Allegro

Adagio

Adagio

ALLEMANDA
Allegro

Allegro